Anacondas

by Rachel Grack

BELLWETHER MEDIA • MINNEAPOLIS, MN

Note to Librarians, Teachers, and Parents:

Blastoff! Readers are carefully developed by literacy experts and combine standards-based content with developmentally appropriate text.

Level 1 provides the most support through repetition of high-frequency words, light text, predictable sentence patterns, and strong visual support.

Level 2 offers early readers a bit more challenge through varied simple sentences, increased text load, and less repetition of high-frequency words.

Level 3 advances early-fluent readers toward fluency through increased text and concept load, less reliance on visuals, longer sentences, and more literary language.

Level 4 builds reading stamina by providing more text per page, increased use of punctuation, greater variation in sentence patterns, and increasingly challenging vocabulary.

Level 5 encourages children to move from "learning to read" to "reading to learn" by providing even more text, varied writing styles, and less familiar topics.

Whichever book is right for your reader, Blastoff! Readers are the perfect books to build confidence and encourage a love of reading that will last a lifetime!

This edition first published in 2019 by Bellwether Media, Inc.

No part of this publication may be reproduced in whole or in part without written permission of the publisher. For information regarding permission, write to Bellwether Media, Inc., Attention: Permissions Department, 6012 Blue Circle Drive, Minnetonka, MN 55343.

Library of Congress Cataloging-in-Publication Data

Names: Koestler-Grack, Rachel A., 1973- author.
Title: Anacondas / by Rachel Grack.
Description: Minneapolis, MN : Bellwether Media, Inc., 2019. |
    Series: Blastoff! Readers. Animals of the Rain Forest | Audience: Ages 5-8. |
    Audience: K to grade 3. | Includes bibliographical references and index.
Identifiers: LCCN 2018031000 (print) | LCCN 2018036934 (ebook) |
    ISBN 9781681036717 (ebook) | ISBN 9781626179479 (hardcover : alk. paper)
Subjects: LCSH: Anaconda--Juvenile literature. | Rain forest animals--Juvenile literature.
Classification: LCC QL666.O63 (ebook) | LCC QL666.O63 K64 2019 (print) | DDC 597.96/7--dc23
LC record available at https://lccn.loc.gov/2018031000

Editor: Betsy Rathburn   Designer: Jeffrey Kollock

Printed in the United States of America, North Mankato, MN

Table of Contents

Life in the Rain Forest

Anacondas are huge snakes **adapted** to live in the rain forests of South America.

This hot **biome** is home to many animals. Anacondas are some of the biggest!

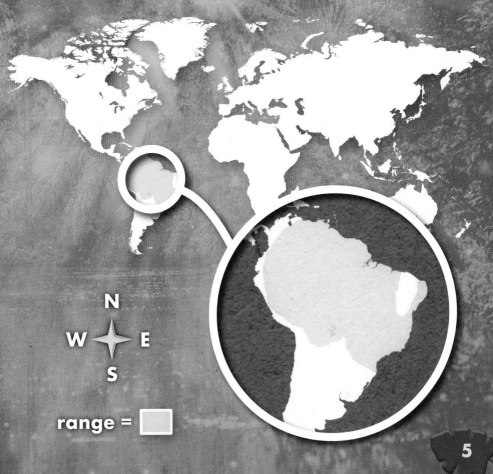

Green Anaconda Range

N
W • E
S

range = ☐

Spotted skin helps anacondas hide from **prey**. They creep through tall grasses.

They twist through rivers and **marshes**. Surprise attack!

Anacondas spend a lot of time swimming.

nostril

Special Adaptations

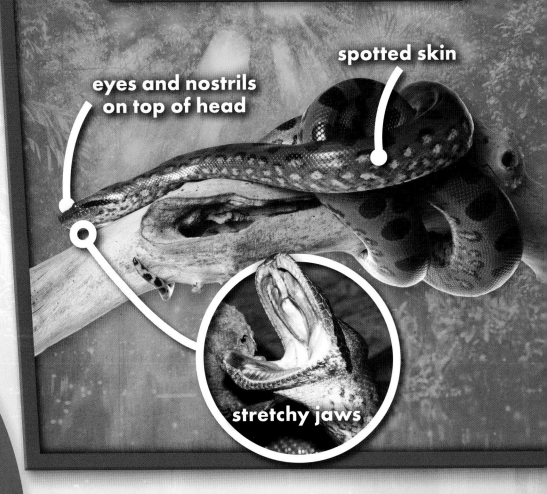

spotted skin

eyes and nostrils
on top of head

stretchy jaws

The snakes stay **alert**
while underwater.
Their eyes and **nostrils**
are on top of their heads!

Rain Forest Survival

Rain forests have
wet and dry seasons.
Some anacondas bury
themselves in mud
during the dry season.

They may **hibernate**
there until it rains again.

Green Anaconda Stats

Least Concern	Near Threatened	Vulnerable	Endangered	Critically Endangered	Extinct in the Wild	Extinct

conservation status: least concern

life span: up to 10 years

hibernating

The rain forest is very large. Anacondas use their tongues to **navigate**!

They flick their forked tongues to smell for food and find **mates**.

female
with mates

13

Rain forests are very wet places. Anacondas have loose skin that holds extra water.

Thick, strong bodies make them great swimmers and divers.

Stretchy Jaws

Anacondas wait in water for prey to come near. Then, they strike!

These **constrictors** eat foods such caimans and deer. They wrap around and squeeze prey.

constricting

After the kill, anacondas open wide. Stretchy **ligaments** hold their jaws together.

This helps them swallow their food whole!

Anaconda Diet

green iguanas

tapirs

capybaras

Anaconda skin stretches to fit prey.
Big meals slow them down.

They sometimes throw up their last meal to make a quick getaway. But little scares this rain forest **predator**!

Glossary

adapted—well suited due to changes over a long period of time

alert—ready for action

biome—a large area with certain plants, animals, and weather

constrictors—snakes that squeeze food to kill it

hibernate—to spend a long time in deep sleep

ligaments—bands of tissue that hold bones together

marshes—low, wet lands

mates—partners

navigate—to find the way from place to place

nostrils—the two openings of the nose

predator—an animal that hunts other animals for food

prey—animals hunted by other animals for food

To Learn More

AT THE LIBRARY
Golkar, Golriz. *Anacondas*. Minneapolis, Minn.: Pop, 2018.

Hansen, Grace. *Green Anacondas*. Minneapolis, Minn.: Abdo Kids, 2017.

Statts, Leo. *Anacondas*. Minneapolis, Minn.: Abdo Zoom, 2017.

ON THE WEB

FACTSURFER

Factsurfer.com gives you a safe, fun way to find more information.

1. Go to www.factsurfer.com.

2. Enter "anacondas" into the search box.

3. Click the "Surf" button and select your book cover to see a list of related web sites.

Index

The images in this book are reproduced through the courtesy of: cellistka, front cover, p. 1; robertharding/ Alamy, pp. 4-5; Toniflap, p. 6; Fernando Flores/ Wikipedia, pp. 6-7; Foto Arena LTDA/ Alamy, pp. 8-9; petographer/ Alamy, pp. 9, 22; chamleunejai, p. 9; Biosphoto/ SuperStock, pp. 10, 10-11; CORDIER Sylvain/ Hemis/ Super Stock, pp. 12-13; M. Watsonantheo/ Pantheon/ SuperStock, p. 13; Nature Picture Library/ Alamy, p. 14; Franco Banfi, pp. 14-15; Patrick K. Campbell, p. 16; J.-M. Labat & F. Rouquette/ Biosphoto, pp. 16-17; Arco Images GmbH/ Alamy, pp. 18-19; Poul Riishede, p. 19 (top left); Ben Queenborough, p. 19 (top right); Kevin Xu Photography, p. 19 (bottom); Francois Gohier/ SuperStock, pp. 20-21; David Persson, p. 21; petographer/ Alamy, p. 22.